MONROEVILLE PUBLIC LIBRARY
4000 Gateway Campus Blvd.
Monroeville, PA 15146

OVIRAPTOR

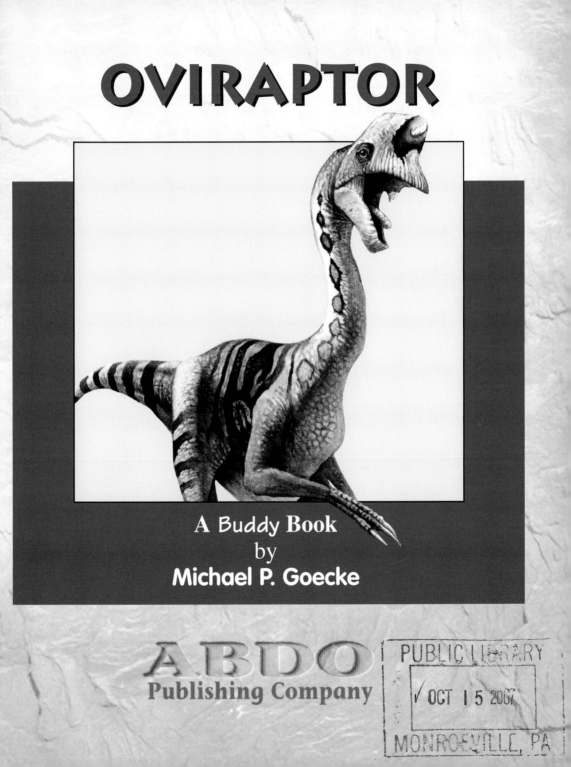

A Buddy Book
by
Michael P. Goecke

ABDO
Publishing Company

PUBLIC LIBRARY

✓ OCT 1 5 2007

MONROEVILLE, PA

J
567.96

VISIT US AT

www.abdopublishing.com

Published by ABDO Publishing Company, 4940 Viking Drive, Edina, Minnesota 55435.

Copyright © 2007 by Abdo Consulting Group, Inc. International copyrights reserved in all countries. No part of this book may be reproduced in any form without written permission from the publisher. Buddy Books™ is a trademark and logo of ABDO Publishing Company.

Printed in the United States.

Edited by: Sarah Tieck
Graphic Design: Denise Esner
Cover Art: ©Julius T. Csotonyi, title page
Interior Photos/Illustrations: Page 5: Joe Tucciarone; pages 6, 7, 8, 18 & 25: Natural History Museum; pages 10, 15 & 16: Photos.com; Pages 12 & 21: ©Julius T. Csotonyi; page 14: Pro Litho; page 23: American Museum of Natural History.

Library of Congress Cataloging-in-Publication Data

Goecke, Michael P., 1968-
    Oviraptor / Michael P. Goecke
        p. cm. — (Dinosaurs)
    Includes index.
    ISBN-13: 978-1-59928-698-3
    ISBN-10: 1-59928-698-X
    1. Oviraptor—Juvenile literature. I. Title.

QE862.S3G645 2007
567.912—dc22
                                                    2006031421

TABLE OF CONTENTS

 WHAT WAS IT?

Millions of years ago, the world was a very different place. There were no buildings or people. At that time, dinosaurs walked the planet.

One of these dinosaurs was the Oviraptor. The Oviraptor was a meat-eating dinosaur. It lived about 80 million years ago, during the Late **Cretaceous** period.

The Oviraptor was not a large dinosaur. It was about six feet (two m) long and weighed up to 76 pounds (35 kg).

Oviraptor
OH-vuh-RAP-tuhr

The Oviraptor was part of a special group of dinosaurs called theropods. Theropods stood on their back legs and usually had sharp teeth.

TAIL

LEG

FOOT

HEAD

ARM

The Oviraptor did not have sharp teeth. But, it did walk on two legs.

Scientists think the Oviraptor could run very fast on its strong legs. It used its speed to escape **predators**. And, its tail helped it balance while running.

WHY WAS IT SPECIAL?

The Oviraptor had a special crest on its head. The crest was hollow and surrounded by thin bone.

Scientists are still exploring how the Oviraptor used its crest.

Some scientists think the Oviraptor used its crest to make noise. This noise might have been used to call other Oviraptors. Or, the Oviraptor may have used the noise to warn other Oviraptors of danger.

Other scientists say the crest might have helped the Oviraptor stay warm or cool. African elephants cool their blood with their ears. They flap their ears to cool the blood flowing through them. As the blood moves through the body, it cools the elephant.

African elephants flap their large ears to help them stay comfortable in the hot sun.

The Oviraptor may have used its giant crest in a similar way. On a cool day, the sun could have warmed both the Oviraptor's crest and the blood that flowed through it. This in turn would have helped warm the Oviraptor's body.

It is even possible that the Oviraptor's crest was brightly colored. Perhaps this coloring impressed other members of its **species**. Still, no one knows for sure.

A brightly colored crest may have made the Oviraptor look beautiful to other Oviraptors.

Oviraptor **fossils** have been found in what is now Mongolia, in central Asia. The fossils show that the Oviraptor lived during the Late **Cretaceous period**. This was about 80 million years ago.

At this time, the world was warmer. There was a cold season and a warm season. But, there was no ice at the North and South poles. And, the land was covered with forests and flowering plants.

WHAT DID IT EAT?

The Oviraptor may have stolen other dinosaur eggs to eat.

Oviraptor means "egg stealer." The Oviraptor got this name because, for many years, scientists believed Oviraptors stole and ate eggs from other dinosaurs.

Today, scientists are less sure about what Oviraptors ate. Newer **fossil** findings suggest that Oviraptors ate more than just eggs.

Unlike many theropods, the Oviraptor did not have sharp teeth. Instead, it had a beak with no real teeth. It just had one peg-like tooth that hung down from the roof of its mouth. This type of mouth tells scientists that the Oviraptor may have eaten clams and other mollusks.

The Oviraptor's mouth was perfect for opening clams.

The Oviraptor's jaws were probably very strong. It was most likely an omnivore. This means it ate both plants and animals.

Grizzly bears eat both plants and animals. They are one example of a modern-day omnivore.

The Oviraptor's neighbor was the Protoceratops. The Protoceratops was one of the most common ceratopsian dinosaurs.

A ceratopsian dinosaur is often identified by its large head and bony frill. A frill is a hard plate that covers the neck and back of a ceratopsian's head. Other ceratopsian dinosaurs include Triceratops and Styracosaurus.

The Protoceratops was a dinosaur neighbor of the Oviraptor.

The Protoceratops was about six feet (two m) long and three feet (one m) tall. It weighed about 400 pounds (180 kg).

The Protoceratops was an herbivorous, or plant-eating, dinosaur. Scientists think that they lived in herds or groups. Scientists have also discovered Protoceratop's nests. These **fossilized** nests show the Protoceratops eggs laying in a circle. Scientists think that Protoceratops took very good care of their young, like the Oviraptor.

AMAZING FIND

When scientists discovered the first Oviraptor **fossil** in 1924, they saw something amazing. It looked like the Oviraptor was stealing eggs from a Protoceratops nest!

The Oviraptor's full name is *Oviraptor philoceratops*. This means "raptor that likes to eat ceratopsian eggs."

Almost 70 years later, scientists started to see something different. A **fossil** discovery in 1993 showed that Oviraptors may not have been egg stealers after all. Many scientists now believe the fossilized eggs were actually Oviraptor's own eggs!

Fossil discoveries show that the Oviraptor was very protective of its nest.

Scientists found a **fossil** of a female Oviraptor on her own nest. She had her arms spread out to cover her eggs. Scientists think that the mother died protecting her eggs from a sandstorm. This discovery shows that theropod dinosaurs, such as the Oviraptor, took care of their young.

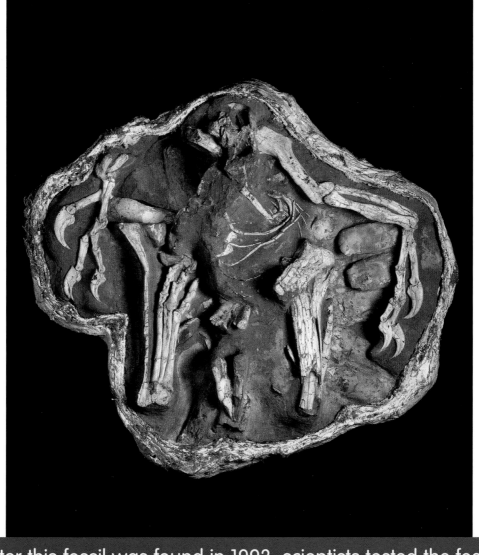

After this fossil was found in 1993, scientists tested the fossil that had been discovered in 1924. The tests proved that both Oviraptors had been protecting their own eggs.

THE OVIRAPTOR FAMILY

The Oviraptor is a distant relative of the Velociraptor. The Velociraptor was a theropod, too. Its name means "quick burglar."

The Velociraptor was six feet (two m) long, but stood only three feet (one m) tall. It had a lightweight body. So, it could run fast to catch its prey. Scientists think the Velociraptor could run up to 40 miles (64 km) per hour!

Unlike the Oviraptor, the Velociraptor was an excellent hunter of other dinosaurs. It had a mouth full of about 80 sharp teeth.

The Velociraptor's other main hunting tools were its speed and a special claw on each foot. This was called the "killing claw." It was located on the second toe of each foot. The claw was curved and four inches (10 cm) long.

The Velociraptor used its teeth and claws to hunt other dinosaurs.

Some scientists say the Velociraptor used its claws to kill its prey. Others think it used them to grab onto and hold its prey. Then, the Velociraptor used its teeth to make the kill. This is similar to what a lion or a tiger does today.

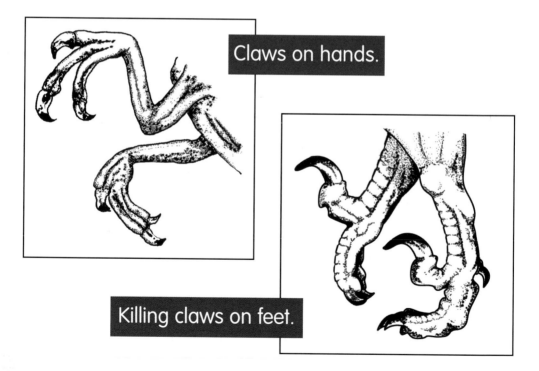

Claws on hands.

Killing claws on feet.

Oviraptor **fossils** were first found in the Gobi Desert in 1924. The Gobi Desert is in Mongolia. A famous **paleontologist** named Henry F. Osborn described and named the Oviraptor.

Osborn led many expeditions in search of fossils. He made several trips into Mongolia and the American West. There, Osborn also helped study other famous dinosaurs. These include the Tyrannosaurus rex and the Velociraptor.

American Museum of Natural History
Central Park West at 79th Street
New York, NY 10024-5192
http://www.amnh.org

The Mongolian State Museum
Ulan Bator, Mongolia

OVIRAPTOR

NAME MEANS	Egg stealer
DIET	Eggs, mollusks
WEIGHT	76 pounds (35 kg)
LENGTH	6 feet (2 m)
TIME	Late Cretaceous period
ANOTHER THEROPOD	Velociraptor
SPECIAL FEATURE	Crest on its head
FOSSILS FOUND	Mongolia

The Oviraptor lived 80 million years ago.

The first humans appeared 1.6 million years ago.

Triassic Period	Jurassic Period	Cretaceous Period	Tertiary Period
245 Million years ago	208 Million years ago	144 Million years ago	65 Million years ago
Mesozoic Era			Cenozoic Era

29

WEB SITES

To learn more about the Oviraptor, visit ABDO Publishing Company on the World Wide Web. Web sites about the Oviraptor are featured on our "Book Links" page. These links are routinely monitored and updated to provide the most current information available.

www.abdopublishing.com

Cretaceous period a period of time that happened 144–65 million years ago.

fossil remains of very old animals and plants commonly found in the ground. A fossil can be a bone, a footprint, or any trace of life.

paleontologist someone who studies very old life, such as dinosaurs, mostly by studying fossils.

predator an animal that hunts and eats other animals.

species a group of animals with many things in common.

INDEX